# TOOLS FOR CAREGIVERS

- **F&P LEVEL:** C
- **WORD COUNT:** 30
- **CURRICULUM CONNECTIONS:** family, relationships

## Skills to Teach

- **HIGH-FREQUENCY WORDS:** are, he, her, his, is, my, she, they, this
- **CONTENT WORDS:** aunt, brother, dad, mom, sister, uncle
- **PUNCTUATION:** periods
- **WORD STUDY:** /aw/, spelled *au* (*aunt*); /k/, spelled *c* (*uncle*); long /a/, spelled *ey* (*they*); long /e/, spelled *y* (*family*); long /i/, spelled *y* (*my*)
- **TEXT TYPE:** information report

## Before Reading Activities

- Read the title and give a simple statement of the main idea.
- Have students "walk" through the book and talk about what they see in the pictures.
- Introduce new vocabulary by having students predict the first letter and locate the word in the text.
- Discuss any unfamiliar concepts that are in the text.

## After Reading Activities

The word "uncle" uses "c" as a hard /k/ sound. What other sounds can "c" make? Draw two columns on the board: /s/ and /k/. Ask readers to say words out loud that either have "c" with a soft /s/ sound, such as "nice," or with a hard /k/ sound, such as "cat." Write each word on the board in its appropriate column. How many words can readers list?

Tadpole Books are published by Jump!, 5357 Penn Avenue South, Minneapolis, MN 55419, www.jumplibrary.com

Copyright ©2025 Jump. International copyright reserved in all countries. No part of this book may be reproduced in any form without written permission from the publisher.

**Editor:** Jenna Gleisner **Designer:** Molly Ballanger

**Photo Credits:** FatCamera/iStock, cover; Andrey_Popov/Shutterstock, 1; SDI Productions/iStock, 2tl, 2mr, 2bl, 3, 4–5, 6–7; kali9/iStock, 2tr, 2ml, 2br, 8–9, 10–11, 12–13; FG Trade Latin/iStock, 14–15; SolStock/iStock, 16.

Library of Congress Cataloging-in-Publication Data
Names: Sterling, Charlie W., author.
Title: Aunts and uncles / by Charlie W. Sterling.
Description: Minneapolis, MN: Jump!, Inc., [2025]
Series: Families | Includes index.
Audience: Ages 3–6
Identifiers: LCCN 2023049859 (print)
LCCN 2023049860 (ebook)
ISBN 9798892130141 (hardcover)
ISBN 9798892130158 (paperback)
ISBN 9798892130165 (ebook)
Subjects: LCSH: Aunts—Juvenile literature. | Uncles—Juvenile literature. | Families—Juvenile literature.
Classification: LCC HQ759.94 .S74 2025 (print)
LCC HQ759.94 (ebook)
DDC 306.87—dc23/eng/20231106
LC record available at https://lccn.loc.gov/2023049859
LC ebook record available at https://lccn.loc.gov/2023049860

FAMILIES

# AUNTS AND UNCLES

by Charlie W. Sterling

## TABLE OF CONTENTS

tadpole
books

# WORDS TO KNOW

aunt

brother

dad

mom

sister

uncle

# AUNTS AND UNCLES

**This is my mom.**

mom's sister

mom

**This is her sister.**

aunt

**She is my aunt.**

7

dad

This is his dad.

dad's brother

dad

**This is his brother.**

11

uncle

12

He is his uncle.

aunt

uncle

14

They are family.

# LET'S REVIEW!

Aunts and uncles are our parents' siblings. Kim and Mal's mom has two sisters. How many aunts do Kim and Mal have?

# INDEX